Do G☺☺D STUFF ™

NEW YORK

The Official Do Good Stuff™ Journal

Published in New York, New York, by Morgan James Publishing. Morgan James and The Entrepreneurial Publisher are trademarks of Morgan James, LLC.

Morgan James Publishing, The Entrepreneurial Publisher
5 Penn Plaza, 23rd Floor, New York City, New York 10001
(212) 655-5470 office • (516) 908-4496 fax
www.MorganJamesPublishing.com

This is a trustworthy saying, and I want you to insist on these teachings so that all who trust in God will devote themselves to doing good. These teachings are good and beneficial for everyone. - Titus 3:8 NLT

9781630479268   paperback
9781630479275   hardcover

Library of Congress Control Number: 2015921108

Cover Design Trademarked by:
Joel Comm

Produced by:
Brittany Bondar

In an effort to support local communities, raise awareness and funds, Morgan James Publishing donates a percentage of all book sales for the life of each book to Habitat for Humanity Peninsula and Greater Williamsburg.

Get involved today, visit
www.MorganJamesBuilds.com

Habitat for Humanity®
Peninsula and
Greater Williamsburg
Building Partner

www.DoGoodStuff.com